Jesus Loves ....

　　　　This I Know

　　Today, ... ,

　　　　And forever

Jesus Loves Me

ANNA B. WARNER, 1820-1915   WILLIAM

...es loves me! this I know,   For the Bi - ble tells
...s me! He who died   Heaven's gate to o -
...me! He will stay   Close be-side me all

...hey are weak but He is strong.
Let His lit - tle child come in.
will hence-forth live for Thee.

Jesus Loves Me
This I Know

The Remarkable Story
Behind The World's Most
Beloved Children's Song

ROBERT J. MORGAN

COUNTRYMAN

NASHVILLE, TENNESSEE

The New King James Version (NKJV) © 1979, 1980, 1982, 1992, Thomas Nelson, Inc., Publisher. Used by permission.
New Century Version® (NCV). Copyright © 1987, 1988, 1991 by Thomas Nelson, Inc. All rights reserved. Used by permission.
The King James Version of the Bible (KJV).
The New Revised Standard Version of the Bible (NRSV), © 1989 by the Division of Christian Education of the National Council of the Churches of Christ in the USA. Used by permission.
The Holy Bible, New Living Translation (NLT) © 1996. Used by permission of Tyndale House Publishers, Inc., Wheaton, Ill. All rights reserved.

Project Editor: Kathy Baker

Designed by Koechel Peterson & Associates, Minneapolis, Minnesota

Photography and images:
Constitution Island Association, Inc. Founded in 1916—pages 2, 10, 11, 14, 16-19, 22, 26, 29, 33, 34, 47, 48, 65, 68, 71, 74, 76, 78, 79, 81, 85
Charles T. Lyle—pages 23, 34-35, 42-43, 48, 62, 68, 72
Mark Cowart—pages 8, 9, 10, 14, 15, 29, 46, 64, 70, 74, 88, 91
National Archives and Records Administration—pages 28, 68, 87.

ISBN 1-4041-0300-7

Printed and bound in the United States of America

www.thomasnelson.com | www.jcountryman.com

www.robertjmorgan.com

"**God loved** the world so much that he gave his one and only Son so that whoever believes in him may not be lost, but have eternal life."

JOHN 3:16 NCV

Jesus Loves Me

WORDS BY ANNA B. WARNER
MUSIC BY WILLIAM B. BRADBURY

Jesus loves me! this I know,

For the Bible tells me so;

Little ones to Him belong,

They are weak, but He is strong.

Jesus loves me! He who died,

Heaven's gate to open wide;

He will wash away my sin,

Let His little child come in.

Jesus take this heart of mine,

Make it pure and wholly Thine;

Thou hast bled and died for me

I will henceforth live for Thee.

Jesus loves me! He will stay,

Close beside me all the way;

He's prepared a home for me,

And someday His face I'll see.

CHORUS

Yes, Jesus loves me,

Yes Jesus loves me,

Yes, Jesus loves me,

The Bible tells me so.

Note: The words to two of Anna Warner's original verses were a little bit different from what we sing today. For the original lyrics, please see page 55.

Cristo me ama, bien lo sé,
Su palabra me hace ver,
Que los niños son de Aquel,
Quien es nuestro Amigo fiel

Cristo Me Ama

Cristo me ama, pues murió,
Y el cielo me abrió;
Él mis culpas quitará,
Y la entrada me dará.

Cristo me ama, es verdad,
Y me cuida en su bondad,
Cuando muera, si soy fiel,
Viviré allá con Él.

CORO
Cristo me ama,
Cristo me ama,
Cristo me ama,
La Biblia dice así.

BIRTHPLACE OF A BELOVED SONG

A FLAT–BOTTOMED rowboat plowed across the Hudson, bobbing
on the currents, the oars hoisted and pulled by old Buckner, who was
dressed for the occasion in white shirt and suspenders. Behind him the
austere gray stones of United States Military Academy at West Point
climbed skyward, like ramparts of an enormous fortress. On either side, the
savage beauty of the Hudson River Valley hushed the passengers.

The only sound was the gentle splashing of the oars as they cut the water—that, and the groaning of the breeze through the gorge and the occasional cawing of a crow.

Three hundred yards away on the east bank of the Hudson, a slender elderly woman awaited the passengers. She was dressed in a voluminous, outdated silk dress with small flowering patterns. A paisley shawl was draped around her shoulders, and a large black ribbon encircled her graying hair, which was parted in the middle and pushed back from a deeply–lined face that caught and reflected the summer sunshine. Pitchers of lemonade sat in her kitchen and the sweet

Jesus loves me, this I kn

aroma of gingerbread wafted through the old house.

Scattered with artistic randomness around the property were flower gardens, grape arbors, raspberry bushes, and vegetable plots. Beyond the grounds, little pathways disappeared into the hemlock and pine forest.

for the bible tells me so.

One by one, the young men disembarked and jaunted up the flowery pathway toward the house, escaping the confinement of their duties for a rare afternoon of refreshment. These sturdy West Point Cadets were coming to study the Bible with the far-famed author of a song they had known from childhood: *Jesus loves me, this I know, for the Bible tells me so.*

This is the remarkable story of Anna Warner, and her sister, Susan. It's a riches-to-rags tale of patriotism and faith featuring a cast of characters that includes Manhattan publishers, West Point Cadets, two peculiar gray-haired women, an American president, a family of Christian heroes, one black sheep, and millions of children around the world.

But my life is worth nothing
unless I use it for doing the work
assigned me by the Lord Jesus—
the work of telling others the
Good News about God's
wonderful kindness and love.

ACTS 20:24 NLT

Settling Down in Canaan

THE WARNERS were a notable family in American history. The first members of the clan came to the New World in 1637, sailing aboard the *Globe* and landing in Ipswich, Massachusetts. Succeeding generations of Warners moved down to Connecticut and on to New York, where some of them settled in the town of Canaan.

Wherever the Warners were, they gained reputations as patriots and community leaders. Six of the Warners fought in the Revolutionary

War alongside George Washington, and the family later came into the possession of Gilbert Stuart's famous portrait of Washington, which became their most prized possession and a symbol of their commitment to America.

Jason Warner, who fought with distinction in the War of Independence, had four sons, two of which enter our story. Thomas, the oldest sibling, was born in Canaan in 1784. Unfortunately, he was something of a black sheep, and he caused his kin continual anxiety. Instead of embracing the family's patriotism, for example, he skipped to Europe during the War of 1812.

Thomas Warner

When Thomas returned he became an Episcopal priest, and though his religious passions ran shallow, Thomas managed to be appointed chaplain at West Point Military Academy, a post he filled with debatable distinction for ten years. He wasn't good at following directions or regulations, he was frequently absent, and it's said he often used other people's sermons without giving them credit. He married for money, then bitterly complained when his wife lost the money for which he had married her. Dismissed from his job at West Point in 1838, Thomas returned to Europe where he wandered about sponging off friends until he landed in debtor's prison, dying there in

According to the Warner Archives ("Warner Family Papers 1800–1916"), Henry Warner gave seven oil paintings in exchange for the Stuart portrait, and it became a symbol of the family's patriotism. The Stuart portrait was Anna and Susan Warner's most cherished possession, and it meant more to them than anything else on earth, including Constitution Island. They once had to give it to a judge as a loan on account of financial indebtedness, but he kept it securely for them. When Susan Warner wrote *The Wide Wide World* in 1850, the judge returned it. It hung over their fireplace throughout their lives, and the Warners saved it for the Cadets at West Point. The original painting now resides in a gallery of the West Point Museum, and a copy hangs over the mantle of the Warner House on Constitution Island.

1848. He was buried in a pauper's grave in Paris.

Thomas Warner did one very good thing, however. While at West Point he persuaded his brother Henry to buy 280 acres of real estate situated just across the Hudson River. It was dubbed Constitution Island. The two brothers dreamed of building a resort there, complete with a castle-themed hotel.

Henry Warner was just the man to undertake such a project. As an attorney in New York City, he had worked in the law offices of Robert Emmet before establishing his own practice in 1814. Three years later, he married Anna Marsh Bartlett, a socialite from a well-heeled family. The Warners were rising stars in the city's social and commercial life, and as Henry's

Henry Warner

DESIGN FOR A CASTLE HOTEL ON CONSTITUTION ISLAND, OPPOSITE WEST POINT.

income grew, he dabbled in business ventures and real estate. His name was bandied about by the legislators at the State House in Albany, and his future seemed bright[1].

The Warners were rising stars in the city's social and commercial life

Then sorrow paid a visit. Henry's devoted wife, the frail Anna, died in 1826 after the birth of the couple's fifth child. Three of the children also passed away before reaching adulthood. Henry's sister, Frances, better known as Aunt Fanny, age 23, became a second mother to the remaining children—two precocious sisters named Susan and Anna.

Anna Marsh Bartlett

The two girls were Henry's pride and joy, and he gave them the best possible education under the watchful eye of gifted tutors[2]. In addition to mathematics, history, French, Latin, and music, the girls also learned sewing, drawing, painting, and storytelling, and they frequently joined in the activities of the Mercer Street Presbyterian Church.

When their Uncle Thomas suggested Henry purchase Constitution Island, the family checked it out together. Their first visit seemed none too promising, at least not to Susan. It was a tree-laden rock on the Hudson about fifty miles above New York City, and here's what she wrote in her journal on July 28, 1834:

This morning we all took the boat and rowed over to Constitution Island. We wandered about looking at the prospect, and considering the ground, for Father actually had thought of buying it for a country place. It did not look very prepossessing, however; for nothing can be more rough and rude than the face of that island.[3]

Although Constitution Island was undeveloped, there was a simple white-framed house, portions of which dated from the American Revolution. The walls of the house were very thick, and the windows in the sitting room and dining room were set deeply into the wall and

According to the guide at West Point, Constitution Island received its name in colonial times, not in honor of the American constitution but in honor of the British constitution. Furthermore, the Warners often referred to the island as "Martlaers Rock." Anna explained she had once been told that a French family named Martlaer had lived there, although other explanations for the name have been offered as well.[4]

had wide sills. These walls, the family was told, originally served as barracks for colonial troops.

Henry purchased the land in 1836. Hiring a crew of builders, he quickly expanded the house with a Victorian wing consisting of eight rooms. He intended the house to become the servants' quarters for the lavish summer home he planned to build for himself on a nearby plot. He also hired New York architect A. J. Davis to draw up plans for a hotel. He visualized an exclusive resort, and the project was excitedly discussed in the New York papers.

DISASTER

THE NEXT YEAR, 1837, Henry's high-flying world crashed. America had been walloped with a financial panic and a lingering depression. Henry watched helplessly as his investments soured, his assets disappeared, his wealth evaporated, and his debt mushroomed. The cook, maids, coachman, gardener, and tutors were let go[5]. Forced to sell his elegant home on St. Mark's Place in New York City, Henry moved his family in 1838 into his newly renovated house on Constitution Island.

Anna was thirteen years old at the time, and Susan was eighteen when they had this rude awakening. Gone were the piano, the fine wardrobe and finely-tooled furniture, the expansive rooms of their city home blessed with paintings and possessions and prestige. Gone were the servants and most of the silverware. Gone, the bustling streets of New York City. Suddenly the little family found itself in a drafty old house on a deserted island, neck–deep in debt.

Henry never fully recovered, either financially or emotionally. He tried farming the island, draining the marshes and digging ditches and planting potatoes. He erected a grape arbor, raised pigs and fowl, and sold crops. In his spare time, he tried to practice law and he resumed buying and selling property. But this meant borrowing more money, and his finances went from bad to worse. Eventually the sheriff seized the family's remaining treasures to be sold at auction, and the Warners were left with a virtually empty house. In response, Anna went out, found some wildflowers, put them in a vase, and suggested everyone try to make the best of it.

Wanting to help, the two sisters worked hard chopping

wood and raising vegetables, yet nothing could spoil their childlike love for the island. Their lives were tinged with a certain idyllic color, like the sparkle of a springtime sunrise on the cold waters of the Hudson. They rowed on the river, picked wildflowers among the rocky slopes of the island, planted gardens, tended grapes, studied birds and wildlife, sketched and drew, and gazed at the somber bulwarks of West Point across the river.

Perhaps the constant sight of those towering gray walls reminded them they were living on hallowed ground. Some historians have gone so far as to say that in many ways our country and its defenses began on Constitution Island[6]. The first mention of George Washington in any act or resolution of Congress was when he was appointed a member of the committee to report on the possible defensive measures that should be assembled on the Hudson River at the point of Constitution Island.

Consequently, on April 30, 1778, fearing British ships would slip up the Hudson to attack New York, Revolutionary forces suspended a

PLAN
OF
WEST POIN

massive chain from the island to the opposite bank. Each two-foot link in the chain weighed 125 pounds, and cannons mounted on the island could attack enemy vessels rounding Gees Point[7]. Benedict Arnold tried to sabotage this chain by removing a link in 1780, but it held secure. Thus the Northeast was protected from British incursion through the Hudson Valley for the duration of the war. The great staples that secured the chain to the rocks on the island are still visible today. To both Gen. George Washington and King George III, this rocky crag in the Hudson was the key to the continent.[8] And it was here, in 1783, that Washington's Life Guards (his bodyguards) were mustered on what is called to this day "Washington's Parade Ground."

LIFE CHANGE

WITH SUCH A RICH PATRIOTIC HISTORY, it's not surprising that Constitution Island grew sacred to the Warner sisters as they explored every square foot of it. Perhaps it was the beauty of the land, or the solemn cliffs of West Point, or the star-spangled skies above their heads, but for whatever reason, the girls' hearts turned toward God.

Susan and Anna determined to give their lives without reservation to the Lord Jesus Christ, and in 1841, they sealed that commitment by becoming covenanting members of their dad's church, Mercer Street Presbyterian in New York City. Soon they were head-over-heels in Bible study, first as students then as teachers. They began distributing Christian literature and speaking of their faith to others. They came to know their Bibles frontward and backward, memorizing large amounts of Scripture.

Susan's personally adopted motto was: "Life is to do the will of God."[9]

On one occasion, writing to her friend Mrs. John Bigelow after a serious conversation on the subject of the Lord Jesus, Susan wrote:

"Let me add now one word to it—only to give you my testimony, that nothing in all the world is so good as the knowledge and love of Christ, and no pleasure that can be enjoyed equal to the joy of serving Him with all one's heart. As long as religion stops short of that, it may be duty and it may be ceremony, or it may be fear—but it is not joy and peace. Whoever will let Christ have the whole—heart and life and all—he finds what it means to be rich and glad, with a gladness that nothing can spoil and nothing earthly can take away. I would you might know this joy! I have been learning to know more and more of it for many a year, growing brighter and sweeter as the years went by."[10]

Susan Warner

"Let me a__ now one word to it—only
to give you m__ testimony, that
nothing in all ___ world is so good as
the knowledge an__ __ove of Christ, and
no pleasure that can __e enjoyed equal to
the joy of serving Hi__ with all one's
heart. As long as __ __ __ stops short
of that, it may be __ __ __ __ it may
ceremony, or it m__ __ __ __ __ it
not joy and peace. __ __ __
Christ have the wha__ __
__ __ds wha__

THE WIDE, WIDE WORLD

ℭHRISTIANITY SENT the girls' hearts and creativity a'soaring. Susan created fantasy worlds all her own, and she entertained family and friends with stories assembled in the chambers of her mind. She had a keen ability to rattle off vivid spellbinders, and one day in the old dining room as they finished tea, Aunt Fanny

looked up from collecting the dishes and said, "Sue, you love to read so much; I believe you could write a book if you put your mind to it."[11]

Susan made no reply, but the idea took root in her mind.

The Warners' bookshelves

...AS GOD OFTEN DOES, HE OPENED A WINDOW THAT WOULD LEAD TO MANY OPEN DOORS.

Soon she put pen to paper and discovered she enjoyed writing very much. Before long, she was creating a novel, writing much of it in the old house on the island, and other portions while visiting New York. When Susan read chapters to her family, they raved about it, and her father shopped the manuscript around the publishing circles in New York, believing it was the answer to the family's debt.

No one was interested. This was anguishing for Henry Warner, for he had no other plan to save his island from foreclosure. Being a devout Presbyterian, he persistently asked the Lord for an open door. And as God often does, He opened a window that would eventually lead to many open doors.

It happened when publishing mogul George P. Putnam took the

manuscript to his mother on Staten Island. She was captivated with it, and she told Putnam that if he never published another book he must publish that one. Susan was promptly summoned to Staten Island where she spent several weeks revising her story and correcting proofs. In 1851 *The Wide, Wide World* was published in two volumes under the pseudonym Elizabeth Wetherell.

It did poorly at first. Sales were slow, and Mr. Putnam muttered, "I am not sure whether or not I have made a mistake in accepting it." Within a few years, however, *The Wide, Wide World* was in bookstores everywhere. Susan's novel became the first book written by an American to sell one million copies[12]. Its popularity during the Civil War era was exceeded only by *Uncle Tom's Cabin*.

While the success of *The Wide, Wide World* enabled the Warners to pay some bills and hang onto their island, Susan never received adequate

SUSAN'S NOVEL
BECAME THE FIRST
BOOK WRITTEN BY AN
AMERICAN TO SELL
ONE MILLION COPIES.
ITS POPULARITY
DURING THE CIVIL
WAR WAS EXCEEDED
ONLY BY *UNCLE
TOM'S CABIN*.

compensation for her work; nor did Anna. In those days, copyrights were not enforced, and anyone could print and sell copies without benefit to the author. In fact, despite writing 106 books between them, the two sisters never escaped the ragged nets of poverty. Books were widely pirated at the time, and often because of urgent financial pressure, the sisters sold the rights to their books for immediate cash. Overseas editions brought no royalties at all.

This produced incredible pressure on the sisters to keep churning out books. Until her death, Susan published at least one book a year.[13] Having no funds to travel, the

Warners purchased travel tomes and collected books on history, geography, and science. They also window–shopped in New York City stores that specialized in photographs. Sometimes they would spend an entire morning gazing through stereoscopes at pictures of places they would never visit, fixing the scenes in their memories for inclusion in their books, and they purchased stereoscope views as often as they could afford to do so. This enabled them to describe settings with uncanny accuracy.

The public loved it, and the Warner sisters helped pioneer the field of modern Christian fiction, for the truth of Scripture shone through all their plots and pages.

JANUARY

Pines, ef you're blue, are the best friends I know,
They mope an' sigh an' shiver your feelin's so.

Lowell.

I THINK it is not common to choose this month for a visit to Fairyland. Yet, as you never do thoroughly know people unless you have lived with them, so neither do you well appreciate Fairyland unless...

40   *GARDENING BY MYSELF.*

considering; and if the digging waits a little, the hardy perennials will have their heads above ground, and so miss the chance of being decapitated by your spade; and many self-sown annuals will spring up, ready to your hand for transplanting. And besides,—a matter of much importance where you do your own digging,—the labour will be not half, if the ground is dry and crumbly and *friable*; if it works well, as experts say.

Do you do your own digging?—and do you know how? It is such pretty work, and by no means so tiresome as hoeing.

Susan's next two-volume novel, *Queechy*, was published in 1852, and afterward came a string of books including *Carl Krinken: His Christmas Stocking* (1854), *The Hills of Shatemuc* (1856), *The Old Helmet* (1863), *Melborne House* (1864), and several others. Her last book, *Diana*, was published by Putnam in 1877.

Meanwhile, Anna also was busy with literary projects—and not just books. Her first claim to fame was for inventing a children's game entitled Robinson Crusoe's Farmyard, published in the late 1840s, in which pictures of various animals were painted on white cards. (Both sisters drew and colored the pictures.) The game was sold for years by G. P. Putnam.

Anna's first novel was *Dollars and Cents*, published under the pseudonym Amy Lothrop in 1852. It described the hardships endured by a family who lost their property and all the things dearest to them. Anna obviously drew inspiration from her own experiences, such as an incident in which she and Susan took one of their final pieces of silver to Boston where they sold it to purchase a much-needed overcoat for their ailing father.[14]

Anna went on to write twenty-five books, including Christian classics, children's books, and titles dealing with gardening and flowers and homemaking. Some were illustrated with her own line drawings. Her book *Gardening by Myself*, published in 1872, was the first book by an American woman telling women how to grow flowers and vegetables.

The Warners' parlor

A Busy Life

*I*T'S EASY TO VISUALIZE the two sisters rising early and meeting in the modest, dimly-lit parlor of their old house. Before retiring the night before, they carefully laid out their breakfast items and made sure the kindling basket beside the fireplace was filled with wood. Anna generally rose before dawn and started the fire to ward off the morning chill. Afterward Susan came downstairs for hot tea and a cozy breakfast of bread and butter. The sisters then took their respective seats and began writing. The only

 sounds heard for the next several hours were the crackling of the flames in the hearth, an occasional coal falling through the grate, and the furious scratching of pens to paper. Overhead, the portrait of George Washington silently gazed down at them from its place above the mantel.

The sisters generally completed their writing by lunch, and the rest of the day was given to chores, errands, entertaining, correspondence, gardening, and a handful of leisure hobbies such as rowing and sketching.

On one side of the house, they could hear the river traffic of the Hudson. On the other side, they could hear the rumble and clickity–clack of trains, literally scores of them every day traveling to and from New York City.

It was a busy life and not an easy one, especially in the blustery winter seasons when the temperatures plunged, the rivers choked with ice, and deep snows blanketed the little island. The Warners' house wasn't well winterized, so the sisters usually closed it down during the coldest months and traveled to nearby Highland Falls. Sometimes, though, they would rent an apartment in New York

City, or they would stay in a cottage next to the West Point Hotel.

The Warners' extensive book collection was housed in portable glass–fronted bookshelves that could be secured and taken along with the baggage. Built by a local carpenter, these unique shelves had glass fronts that could be secured, as well as sturdy handles for carrying. One particular bookcase was set aside for all the volumes the sisters had authored.[15] The two women also took their indoor plants, and it was quite a sight to see them relocating every fall, packing their rowboat with their foliage, suitcases, and bookshelves for the trip across the Hudson to catch the train or steamboat.

The Warners' boat and dogs

JESUS LOVES ME

IN 1860, Susan and Anna coauthored a novel entitled *Say and Seal*. The book is an old-fashioned Victorian narrative—sweet, sentimental, and long. The story involved the romance between a school teacher named Endicott Linden and a lovely local girl named Faith Derrick whom he led to faith in Christ. The title is derived from a Puritan expression meaning something like "As good as his word," and few modern readers would have the patience to plow through it even if they could find an unabridged copy.

SAY AND SEAL.

BY

THE AUTHOR OF "WIDE WIDE WORLD,"

AND

THE AUTHOR OF "DOLLARS AND CENTS."

IN TWO VOLUMES.

"If any man make religion as twelve, and the world as thirteen, such a one hath not the spirit of a true New Englandman."—HIGGINSON.

Among the characters in *Say and Seal* is Johnny Fax, a little fellow whose life was very hard. His mother was dead and his feeble–minded father was trying to hold the family together. Johnny was smaller than other children, and he was overlooked frequently until Mr. Linden took a fatherly interest in him. We encounter Johnny Fax early in the novel as a group of children meet Mr. Linden for an outdoor class:

> "Tallest among the group sat Mr. Linden, and all around him—in various attitudes of rest or attention—a dozen boys basked in the sunshine . . . Little Johnny Fax, established in Mr. Linden's lap, divided his attention pretty evenly between the lesson and the teacher; though indeed to his mind the separate interests did not clash."[16]

Later one of the boys spoke to Faith Derrick, saying:

> "You can't think of what Mr. Linden's been to Johnny, Miss

Faith, and to all of us. But he's taken such good care of him, in school and out. It was only last week Johnny told me he liked coming to school in the winter, because then Mr. Linden always went home with him. And whenever he could get in Mr. Linden's lap he was perfectly happy. And Mr. Linden would let him, sometimes, even in school, because Johnny was so little and not very strong—and he'd let him sit in his lap and go to sleep when he got tired, and then Johnny would go back to his lessons as bright as a bee… He's loved Mr. Linden with all his heart."[17]

Then one bitter February day, little Johnny fell sick—"no one just knew

"He's a sick child," said the doctor, shaking his head. "Has the creature nobody to take care of him?" Yes, replied Endicott, he has me.

how; nor just what to do with him—except to send Mr. Linden word by one of the other boys."[18] Mr. Linden fetched the town doctor, and the two men rode to the rundown Fax homestead where they found little Johnny languishing in bed, wrapped in an old plaid cloak, burning with fever. Mr. Linden held Johnny as Dr. Harrison examined him. "He's a sick child," said the doctor, shaking his head. "Has the

creature nobody to take care of him?"

Yes, replied Endicott, he has me.

"It was a night of steady watching—broken by

many other things, but not by sleep. There

was constantly some little thing to do for

the sick child—ranging from giving him a

drink of water, to giving him 'talk,' or

rocking and—it might be—singing

him to sleep. But the restless little

requests never had to wait for their answer and with the whole house sunk in stillness or sleep, Mr. Linden played the part of a most gentle and efficient nurse."[19]

The boy's condition remained unchanged for several days with Dr. Harrison growing increasingly grave. "He is not worse," commented the doctor, "except that not to be better is to be worse." It then became evident the fevered boy was dying. Mr. Linden, with trembling heart, took Johnny in his arms and paced, calming the child and soothing his fears. On one occasion, Johnny tried to talk, but only one word was understandable: "Sing." Walking back and forth in the humble room, the torrid little body in his arms, Mr. Linden began singing in a tone as soft as his footsteps:

Jesus loves me, this I know,
For the Bible tells me so:
Little ones to Him belong,
They are weak, but He is strong.

Jesus loves me, He who died
Heaven's gates to open wide;
He will wash away my sin,
Let his little child come in.

Jesus loves me, loves me still,
Though I'm very weak and ill;
From His shining throne on high
Comes to watch me where I lie.

Jesus loves me, He will stay
Close beside me all the way.
Then his little child will take
Up to heaven for His dear sake.[20]

LITTLE JOHNNY'S DEATH TOUCHED THE NATION, AND THOUSANDS OF PEOPLE MARVELED AT THE BEAUTY OF MR. LINDEN'S DEATHBED SONG. BUT, OF COURSE, NO ONE COULD SING IT.

Those simple words soothed the boy, and Mr. Linden softly placed him in bed. Shortly afterward, with Faith Derrick present, Johnny asked Mr. Linden, "Read about heaven—what you used to." Taking the Bible from a nearby table, the teacher read to the boy from Revelation 21, about the New Jerusalem with its crystal river, golden streets, and gates of pearl. The boy asked about those gates.

"Yes," said Mr. Linden with difficulty. "That is the gate where His little child shall go in! And that is the beautiful city where the Lord Jesus lives, and where my Johnny is going to be with Him forever—and where dear Miss Faith and I hope to come by and by."

The child's hands were folded together, and with a far, pure smile he looked from one face to the other, closing his eyes then in quiet sleep, but with the smile yet left. It was no time for words. The gates of the city seemed too near, where the little traveler's feet were so soon to enter . . . The heaven–light was already shining on that fair face. Faith wiped away tears—and looked—and brushed them away again; but for a long time was very silent. At last she said, very low . . ."Endicott, it seems to me as if I could almost hear them . . . the bells of the city ringing for joy!"

Little Johnny's death touched the nation, and thousands of people marveled at the beauty of Mr. Linden's deathbed song. But, of course, no one could sing it. Miss

OVE DIVINE
what manner of love."

—Countless a - ges
Love the mighty
To n bright, unfa

CHORUS.

as His throne. Love di
rist the Son!
v - er - more.

cv - er - last-ing cho-rus, Praising God, for God

William B. Bradbury

Anna had only composed the words for the novel, not the music. Readers were forced to supply the melody from their own imaginations. (Susan and Anna coauthored *Say and Seal*, but it appears Miss Anna wrote the poem "Jesus Loves Me.")

One of the readers was William Bradbury, who was arguably America's most prolific hymnist. Bradbury had set in motion a great change in American church music, for prior to him most hymns were heavy, noble, and stately. Bradbury preferred lighter melodies that children could sing. His compositions were softer, full of movement, and more singable. He might not have realized that adults would sing his hymns as readily as children, but he paved the way for the era of Gospel music. During his lifetime, fifty–nine separate songbooks appeared under Bradbury's name; and today he is remembered as the musical composer of such favorites as: "He Leadeth Me," "The Solid Rock," "Just as I Am," "Sweet Hour of Prayer" and "Savior, Like a Shepherd, Lead Us."

Bradbury pondered Mr. Linden's song, adjusted the words to make them universally applicable, penned a chorus, and created the simple melody that instantly catapulted "Jesus Loves Me" to stardom as the greatest children's song in history.

"Jesus Loves Me" was only one of the hymns flowing from the little house on Constitution Island. By the late 1800s, American Christians were singing several of the Warners' songs. One of them was inspired by a young minister named Dr. B. M. Adams. One night Dr. Adams trudged home exhausted, having preached at three worship services, conducted Sunday School, led a prayer service and a class meeting, and ministered among his people from early morning till late day. In a letter to Susan Warner, Adams spoke of his fatigue, saying it was one more day's work for Jesus and one less of life for himself. Taking up his words, Miss Susan wrote a poem she sent to him by return mail, "The Song of a Tired Servant." It was later set to music and became a popular hymn in its day under the title "One More Day's Work for Jesus."

One more day's work for Jesus:
In hope, in faith, in prayer,
His Word I've spoken—
His bread I've broken—
To souls faint with despair;
and bade them fell
To Him who hath saved thee.

Jesus loves me
this I know...
for the Bible
tells me so

"The Father himself loves you.
He loves you because you loved
me and believed that I came
from God"

JOHN 16:27 NCV

The Warners' dining room

THE SEASHELL

ESPITE THEIR NOVELS, games, books, sketches, and increasing fame, the Warners never fully recovered from the financial panic of 1837 that plunged their family into indebtedness. Late in her life when she was the last surviving member of her family, Miss Anna lamented to a friend, "Never since I have lived alone have I found it anything like so hard to meet the living expenses, as this winter. Books do not sell in these hard times—Lippincott's January account (her royalties) was almost nothing . . . and everybody wants his money at once!" [21]

Through it all, however, she leaned on the Lord Jesus. One day while sitting with a friend in the old living room, the stress of her

 financial affairs was on her mind. By and by, she rose and took a delicate ocean shell from one of the cases. Holding the shell in her hands, Miss Anna's eyes brimmed with tears as she said, "There was a time when I was very perplexed, bills were unpaid, necessities must be had, and someone sent me this exquisite thing. As I held it I realized that if God could make this beautiful home for a little creature, He would take care of me."

That realization fostered a sense of generosity and hospitality on Constitution Island. The Warner sisters constantly were entertaining others. "My father always trained us that meals were not just eating," Miss Anna once said, "but each one should be a charming ceremony. He would keep the conversation delightful, and yet always at a high level, and kept us from gossip and trivial talk."[22]

As they could, they purchased new silver, grew fresh vegetables, and depended on their handyman, old Buckner, to do the fishing and hunting. One guest remembered "the beautifully set table groaning under its burden of beautiful silver, as well as fried chicken, hot rolls, berries, and thick cream."[23] There were frequent breakfast parties and afternoon teas. Anna tended to the garden, raising vegetables, flowers, berries, and fruits.

"Friday I make cake," Anna wrote a friend, "Saturday afternoon come callers in gray (Cadets); Saturday night any number, up to nine, to tea; and Sunday night finds me a pretty tired person."[24] Her industriousness is evidenced in a poem she wrote on October 1, 1857, entitled "The End of a Weary Day."

> A little too tired for work—
> And without the means to play,
> Here I set in the corner,
> After a weary day.

Willis Buckner

It is not that I have done
     So very much to tell—
It is rather the numberless steps,
     And the many thoughts as well.

First making the cakes for breakfast,
     And then a sketch from the boat
Where far, far down the river,
     Tied fast to a stake, we float.

Then making the pies for dinner,
     And then to Magazine Fort,
Where another sketch might have been finished
     If the rain had not cut it short.

And then digging about the garden—
     Digging and planting out,
And then to drive under cover,
     The feathery chicken rout.

And then came tea and quiet—
     And a bundle of proofs came then;
While darkness covered our dwelling
     And the rain began again.

And now in the chimney corner
　　With my head against the wall,
I sit and have not more spirit
　　For my work at all.

The woodfire flashes gaily
　　But my closed eyes catch no gleam;
And its chipper voice beside me
　　Calls no fairy dream.[25]

No matter how tired, however, the sisters almost always ended each day with evening devotions. One guest recalled, "When bedtime came Bertha (the housekeeper) would join the circle, candles would be lit, and a large-print Bible set before her from which Miss Warner would read a chapter or two before kneeling to pray for us all. I used to wonder how she could remember all the things she prayed about, and many a time I was astounded at some reference to subjects we had discussed during the day."[26]

View of West Point, ca.1860-ca.1865

Chapel & Library, West Point, ca.1860-ca.1865

Little Americans & West Point Cadets

I N October, 1862, the sisters started a new venture, a newspaper just for children entitled *The Little American*. It consisted of fairy tales, animal stories, travel yarns, profiles, and poetry. After months of waiting and uncertainty, they received initial backing for their plans, and it was a labor of love. When the first issues arrived, the women were elated. "Now," said Anna, "may God give His blessing! I do wish it might do well enough to let us go on with it, but the Lord knows best. Perhaps in these hard times it will not even do that—perhaps it will not. I am fond of the little paper—dearly fond, already; nevertheless, let the Lord's will be done."

The paper, which began as a semimonthly publication before being published monthly, required endless study on a wide variety of topics and features crafted with keen imagination. It lasted until December 1864. "Our little paper lived two years," said Anna, "but then, with the pressure of war prices, had to be given up, for we had not capital to risk. It brought us much pleasure and not a cent of loss."[27]

Greater opportunities, however, were just ahead. In 1875 or 1876, not long after the death of their father, a wonderful door opened for the sisters. They were now famous, and the Cadets at West Point knew they lived just across the river. A group of officers' wives asked Susan to teach a Sunday afternoon Bible class, and many of the students wanted to attend. Susan was cautious. "Do you really think the Cadets would like me?" she asked, adding, "It would be a great pleasure to do it."

Anna later described its beginnings: "The first day, there was a very large gathering, curiosity helping on the numbers. After that, it varied from week to week, as must be always, I suppose; especially among

Cadets, where guard duty sometimes interferes; and where Sunday is the free day for seeing friends."

During the winter months, the Bible studies were conducted weekly at the old Cadet Chapel, but the rest of the year they were held on Constitution Island, the Cadets arriving by boat. When Susan wasn't well, Anna substituted. They were quite a sight. Anna had a curl on either side of her face, and the sisters both dressed in old, rustling silk dresses with ruffles at the necks and wrists. These dresses had been cut from the same pattern for forty years,[28] and the sisters looked like displaced characters from one of their own novels. But Susan told her stories in a way that engrossed the Cadets and made her Bible studies very popular, and Anna provided liberal doses of advice and affection. The classes weren't mandatory, but each week large numbers showed up.

The boys took their seats in a semicircle around Susan, and she asked each Cadet to read a Bible verse. Then she opened the Scripture to them for about a half hour until her strength gave out and she closed the lesson.

One of the Cadets recalled: "The visits to Constitution Island were regarded as a great privilege, for not only did they make a break in the severe routine of the daily life, but they enabled the boys to roam further afield than was possible at the Academy, where the restrictions of the cadet limits were pretty irksome to boys accustomed to the free run of the town or country. So the privilege of going to Constitution Island as one of 'Miss Warner's boys' was eagerly sought and highly prized. Every Sunday afternoon during the summer encampment the sisters would send their elderly man . . . He pulled the old flat-bottomed boat across the river to the West Point dock, where the boys with the coveted permits were waiting for him."[29]

"Her English was the best and purest I have ever heard," recalled another Cadet, "and as she went on and her interest grew her eyes shone like stars and her voice became rich and warm . . . She always gave to the boys the brightest and most optimistic side of the faith she loved so well. When she had finished and lay back pale and weary against her cushions her sister, Miss Anna, came down from the house with the rarest treat of the whole week, tea and homemade gingerbread. After that the two sisters and the boys talked over the things of the world that seemed so far from that peaceful quiet orchard. The boys confided their aims and ambitions, and the sisters in the simplest, most unostentatious way sought to implant the right ideals and principles. Miss Warner never forgot any of her boys, and up to the time of her death kept up a correspondence with many of them."

ANNA ALONE

*I*N 1885, Anna and Susan boarded up their home for the winter
and made the short excursion to Highland Falls where they planned
to stay at the cottage of John Bigelow, a friend who spent the winters
elsewhere. While there, Susan became ill and passed away. The funeral
was held in Highland Falls, and the officials at West Point arranged to
bury Susan in the cemetery at the Academy with full military honors, an
unprecedented tribute for a civilian.

Miss Anna later explained: "By special permission of the Secretary of
War, she was laid in the Government cemetery at West Point; there, where
so many of her 'boys' would pass near her; so many at last come back to rest.
From almost at her feet the wooded, rocky ground slopes sharply down to

the river; and beyond that, on the other shore, is . . . Martelaer's Rock—with the old Revolutionary house where so much of her work was done."[30]

After Susan's death, Miss Anna continued the Bible classes alone until her own death in 1915. Much of her work was done quietly while coping with the aches of aging and the sorrows of bereavement. Writing to a friend on April 1, 1886, she said: "How little people know what a ceaseless tide of pain rolls under the quiet surface of my life! The Lord somehow keeps down the waves, and stills the breakers—and yet when people say, 'Come and cheer me up'—I think, how little they know! Some days I seem to do nothing but ache. And yet, Sarah, the quiet is real. Heaven is so much better than earth, and the Lord's will so much sweeter than my own—I am content, content . . ."[31]

A constant stream of Cadets, officers, dignitaries, strangers, reporters, friends, and neighbors paraded up her flower-edged pathway each day. Added to that, bundles of mail arrived each week at the local post office. Some of Anna's greatest blessings were tucked away in those letters and parcels coming from the hundreds of Cadets whose lives had been touched by the sisters through the decades.

> "HEAVEN IS SO MUCH BETTER THAN EARTH, AND THE LORD'S WILL SO MUCH SWEETER THAN MY OWN— I AM CONTENT, CONTENT..."

These "boys" were constantly seeking counsel, requesting prayers, sending gifts, and extending invitations. Anna once wrote, "Some of these boys think they can't get married comfortably unless I look on."[32]

"The winter has gone by like an express train, but loaded as if it had been a freight," Anna said, describing her workload to a friend. "I have been so busy, with two printers at work, and the throng of letters that must not delay . . . They keep me busy, these gray uniforms."[33]

One of her "boys," Col. James L. Lusk, was later ordered back to West

Point, and this time he came with wife in tow. On their first Sunday there, they attended services in the chapel, and afterward, Col. Lusk whispered to his wife to remain seated as others left. He wanted to introduce her to Miss Anna, who was holding a Bible class in the chapel immediately following the morning service. Anna was seated by the pillar with a bonnet tied under her chin, her lined face framed with her trademark curls. Mary Lusk later became a frequent guest to Constitution Island, where the two women sometimes discussed their differences of opinion about religious subjects.

"We have had no fight in a long time," Miss Anna once told her with a smile. "I have a book to read with you that will give us a good occasion for one. Come and read it with me and have a cup of tea."

Mrs. Lusk recalled, "Such invitations were always welcome, and the row across the river to the boat-house on the rock, where

one can still see the staple that held
the end of the cable stretched
across the river from West Point to
ward off the British gunboats, then walk up from
the boat house through the path with its old-fashioned flower borders,
tended by her own hands, to that dear old house nestling in the trees is
one of the precious memories in my life.

"It is hard to give any idea of the atmosphere Miss Anna created
about her. She was strict without harshness, religious without gloom,
narrow-minded as the world counts it, but broad-minded in her
interest in all branches of study . . . The love of all that is beautiful
was a strong element in her character and . . . She would laughingly
say that one of the reasons for the great beauty of the Island was that
her family had never had sufficient means to spoil it."[34]

In all, the Warners taught the Bible to Cadets at West Point for a span of forty years. One of the men, Col. F. W. Altstaetter, described his experiences with Miss Anna:

"When I went to West Point as a cadet in 1893, I was only 17 years of age and accustomed to living in a large family. For the first three years I was there I practically entered no private house except Miss Warner's . . . You can imagine what that meant to me . . . Under date of my first Christmas there I find quite a good bit on the subject, ending as follows: 'I do not like West Point very well, but if it were not for Miss Warner, and of one of my classmates, I'd hate the place as long as I stayed here.'

"My first acquaintance with Miss Warner was when, a bashful, homesick new cadet, feeling very down trodden, I was invited to stay after the regular chapel service on Sunday morning and join her Bible class. She was then a little body, with a wonderfully sweet face crowned with two curls that hung down on each side before her ear. It was one of the saddest faces I ever saw when in repose, but when she smiled it was like a shout of glory with a benediction in it."[35]

A Song Loved Around the World

"Jesus Loves Me" transcends hearts and cultures. Its simple melody and profoundly easy lyrics are known around the world. Many people know the song long before they know the Savior it celebrates.

HERE ARE A FEW OF THE COUNTLESS WAYS IT'S TOUCHED LIVES IN OTHER LANDS.

AMY'S EPIPHANY

AMY CARMICHAEL grew up in a Christian home, but she resisted the Lord's tugging on her heart until a certain church meeting. At the end of the sermon, the speaker told his listeners to sing "Jesus loves me, this I know," and then to be quiet. "During those few minutes, in His great mercy the Good Shepherd answered the prayers of my mother and father and many other loving ones, and drew me, even me, into His fold." Amy went on to become a missionary in India, where she served for fifty-six years without a furlough.

From *Amy Carmichael of Dohnavur*, Frank L. Houghton (Fort Washington, Penn.: Christian Literature Crusade, 1903) p. 36.

for the Bible tells me so.

WHEN THE CHILDREN SING

THE REV. DR. JACOB CHAMBERLAIN, who worked for many years among the Hindus, translated "Jesus Loves Me" into Telugu and taught it to children. A week later he overheard "a little heathen boy, with heathen men and women standing around him, singing [it] at at the top of his voice . . . As he completed the verse someone asked the question: 'Sonny, where did you learn that song?' 'Over at the Missionary School,' was the answer. 'Who is that Jesus, and what is the Bible?' 'Oh! the Bible is the book from God, they say, to teach us how to get to heaven, and Jesus is the name of the divine Redeemer that came into the world to save us from our sins; that is what the missionaries say.' 'Well, the song is a nice one. Come, sing us some more.' And so the little boy went on—a heathen himself, and singing to the heathen—about Jesus and his love. 'That is preaching the Gospel by proxy,' I said to myself, as I turned my pony and rode away, well satisfied to leave my little proxy to tell his interested audience all he himself knew, and sing to them over and over that sweet song of salvation."

From *My Life and the Story of the Gospel Hymns*, Ira D. Sankey, (Philadelphia: P. W. Ziegler Co., 1906) pp. 201-202.

CONSTITUTION ISLAND
FINDS A NEW OWNER

THROUGHOUT THEIR LIVES, the Warner sisters realized that the answer to all their financial needs was literally right at their feet. Constitution Island was an enormous asset, and developers were scurrying to purchase it from the women. But their love for the island and their appreciation for its heritage made such proposals out of the question. They wanted to give the island to West Point to preserve its hallowed history.

But did Uncle Sam want the land? The issue was debated at West Point, in the halls of Congress, and at the White House. On a cold February day in 1903, Anna told her friend Olivia Stokes that some people assumed the government already owned the island, " whereas the prospect is very dim and uncertain that they ever will. Some

Margaret Olivia Sage

Congressman on the Committee fights the purchase as hard as he can, and seems always to gain his point. Perhaps the Lord means me to do something else with it; though as yet I do not see what."[36]

In 1908, through the generosity of a friend named Margaret Olivia Sage, who offered her $150,000 for her home, Anna was able to bequeath Constitution Island to the West Point Military Academy. In a letter dated September 4, 1908, Mrs. Sage wrote to President Theodore Roosevelt, saying, "I take great pleasure in tendering as a gift to the United States from myself and Miss Anna Bartlett Warner, Constitution Island, opposite West Point, embracing about 230 acres of upland and 50 acres of meadow."

Mrs. Sage explained that the Warners could have sold the land at any time, but the family "steadily refused, from patriotic motives, to accept them in order that it might ultimately become a part of the West Point Reservation."

The gift had only one stipulation: that "Miss Warner, who is well advanced in years, may continue to occupy the small part of the island now used by her for the remainder of her life, using her house, grounds, springs, pasture, and firewood as heretofore."

On an early autumn day in 1908, Anna opened her mail to find this letter:

Oyster Bay, N.Y.
September 5, 1908

My dear Miss Warner:

I have written to Mrs. Sage thanking her, and I write to thank you for the singular generosity which has prompted you and her to make this gift to the Nation. You have rendered a real and patriotic service, and on behalf of all our people I desire to express our obligation and our appreciation. With regard, believe me,

Yours sincerely,

Theodore Roosevelt

Anna Warner continued living in the simple white frame house and remained active for the remainder of her life. Even in her eighties, she was often seen rowing her boat around the edges of her island. Then in the fall of 1914, she packed up her belongings, planning to spend the winter in Highland Falls. Friends helped her carry her baggage out the door and down the flowered walkway. As the boat crossed the river, she undoubtedly turned for a final look at the simple white house that had been her home for nearly eighty of her ninety years.

She never returned to the house, for like her sister she passed away in Highland Falls during the winter. Her funeral was conducted in the

old chapel at West Point, Cadets serving as pallbearers. At the cemetery, the entire corps lined up as the bugler played "Taps," after which the coffin was lowered quietly into the ground. At that time, Anna and Susan Warner were the only civilians buried in the military cemetery at West Point, and their graves are located in the far corner beside a stone wall that overlooks their beloved Constitution Island.

Their home is now a museum in their honor, preserved and operated by the Constitution Island Association in cooperation with U. S. Military Academy at West Point. It has changed little since that day when Anna closed the door behind her; and boatloads of tourists show up each summer to walk among Miss Anna's flowers and up and down the little trail from the pier to the house, and to linger in her living room, kitchen, and bedroom.

Part of their precious library still resides in the portable shelves in the family sitting room. Among the titles, visitors can see the devotional classic *Daily Strength for Daily Needs* propped alongside commentaries, Greek and Hebrew reference works, Greek and English concordances, and a myriad of books on history and travel. Their dishes and cooking implements still sit in the kitchen, including the unique sugar–scissors that Susan used each day to divide her sugar cube for tea. The exquisite seashell still sits on its shelf as mute testimony to God's faithfulness. Scattered throughout the house are other gifts sent from around the world by Cadets who never outlived the influence of these two old women who never married but whose sons were legion.

"If there is one thing I give thanks for more than another," Miss Anna once said, "I think it is that the Lord has taught me to love and trust His will above all else. The schooling is hard, but the learning is blessed."[37]

She once said her philosophy of life was expressed by the British

poet George Herbert: "Shine like the sun in every corner."[38]
In one of her precious hymns, Miss Anna wrote:

Lord, I have given my life to Thee,
And every day and hour is Thine—
What Thou appointest let them be:
Thy will is better, Lord, than mine.

Anna Warner lived long enough to realize that had there been no
black sheep, no moments of bereavement, no stock market crash, no
eviction from New York, no financial worries—if there had been none of
those things, there would have been no books, no worldwide ministry, no
thousands of inspired Cadets, and no "Jesus Loves Me."

As visitors pause in the parlor under a copy of Stuart's portrait of
Washington, it isn't difficult to imagine the two sisters rising at dawn,
lighting the fire in the old stone fireplace, whispering a prayer, and sitting

down with a cup of hot tea to begin their day's writing projects. It isn't hard to picture Miss Anna breaking the stillness to say as the fire cracked in the hearth, "Sister, what do you think of this poem? I think it sounds just right for Endicott to sing to little Johnny Fax, don't you?"

And as you stand quietly by the old boathouse while the sun sinks behind the ramparts of West Point, if the breeze is blowing just right, you can still hear the distant chimes from the old Cadet chapel at the entrance to the cemetery high atop the hill across the Hudson, pealing out the notes to that simple, beloved song: "Jesus loves me, this I know; for the Bible tells me so."

Jesus Loves Me

ANNA B. WARNER, 1820   WILLIAM B. BRADBURY, 1816-1868

1. Je-sus loves me! this I know, For the Bi-ble tells me so; Lit-tle
2. Je-sus loves me! he who died Heav-en's gate to o-pen wide; He will
3. Je-sus loves me! he will stay Close be-side me all the way; Thou hast

CHORUS

Jesus Does Love You

The renowned scholar Karl Barth was once asked, "What is the greatest theological discovery you've ever made. He reportedly replied: "Jesus loves me, this I know; for the Bible tells me so."

There is no greater truth. Each of us lives an imperfect life, marked by moral failure and marred by sin. The Bible says, "There is none righteous, no, not one . . . For all have sinned and falls short of the glory of God" (Romans 3:10, 23 NKJV).

Yet the Bible says that Jesus, perfect Man and perfect God, loves us with all His heart. "This is real love," says 1 John 4:10 (NLT). "It is not that we loved God, but that He loved us and sent His Son as a sacrifice to take away our sins."

Romans 5:8 says, "But God demonstrated His own love toward us, in that while we were still sinners, Christ died for us."

"He died for all," says 2 Corinthians 5:15, "that those who live should live no longer for themselves, but for Him who died for them and rose again."

Perhaps the story of "Jesus Loves Me" has left you wanting to become His follower and to begin living, not for yourself, but for the One who loved you. If so, offer this sincere prayer asking Jesus Christ to become your Lord and Savior. Then begin reading your Bible and praying every day, and find a good church this coming Sunday!

Dear Jesus,
Thank you for loving me and for dying for my sins. I confess my faults and failures to You. I believe that Jesus Christ died for me and rose again. I now ask You to become my Savior and the Lord of my life from this day forward. In Jesus' Name I pray. Amen.

Signed: _____ Date: _____

If you've made this prayer, please let me know at www.robertjmorgan.com.

ENDNOTES

1 Olivia Egleston Phelps Stokes, Letters and Memories of Susan and Anna Bartlett Warner (New York: G. P. Putnam's Sons, 1925), p. 13.

2 Olivia Egleston Phelps Stokes, Letters and Memories of Susan and Anna Bartlett Warner (New York: G. P. Putnam's Sons, 1925), p. 13.

3 Quoted in Jesus Loves Me: Incidents from the Life of Anna Bartlett Warner, compiled by Ardis Abbott, published by The Constitution Island Association, 1967.

4 See Olivia Egleston Phelps Stokes, Letters and Memories of Susan and Anna Bartlett Warner (New York: G. P. Putnam's Sons, 1925), pp. 17–18.

5 At Home with Susan and Anna Warner: Receipts and Remembrances from 1836 to 1915, compiled and illustrated by the Constitution Island Association, West Point, NY, 1977, p. 6.

6 Richard de Koster, Constitution Island: American Landmark, published by the Constitution Island Association, Inc., 2003), p. 6.

7 Richard de Koster, Constitution Island: American Landmark, published by the Constitution Island Association, Inc., 2003), p. 9.

8 Richard de Koster, Constitution Island: American Landmark, published by the Constitution Island Association, Inc., 2003), p. 7.

9 Olivia Egleston Phelps Stokes, Letters and Memories of Susan and Anna Bartlett Warner (New York: G. P. Putnam's Sons, 1925), p. 70.

10 Olivia Egleston Phelps Stokes, Letters and Memories of Susan and Anna Bartlett Warner (New York: G. P. Putnam's Sons, 1925), pp. 66–67.

11 Lois Livingston, "West Point, Anna Warner, and 'Jesus Loves Me,'" in Christian Herald (date unknown), p. 24. Also Olivia Egleston Phelps Stokes, Letters and Memories of Susan and Anna Bartlett Warner (New York: G. P. Putnam's Sons, 1925), p. 137.

12 From a document from the Warner Archives entitled "Warner Family Papers 1800–1916, 18 Boxes," p. 2.

13 From a document from the Warner Archives entitled "Warner Family Papers 1800–1916, 18 Boxes," p. 2.

14 Olivia Egleston Phelps Stokes, Letters and Memories of Susan and Anna Bartlett Warner (New York: G. P. Putnam's Sons, 1925), p. 27.

15 See Olivia Egleston Phelps Stokes, Letters and Memories of Susan and Anna Bartlett Warner (New York: G. P. Putnam's Sons, 1925), p. 19.

16 Several editions of Say and Seal were published in two volumes. The words of "Jesus Loves Me" appear on pages 115–116 in volume II.

17 Say and Seal, Vol. II, p. 99.

18 Say and Seal, Vol. II, p. 92.

19 Say and Seal, Vol. II, pp 94–95.

20 Say and Seal, Vol. 2, pp. 115–116.

21 Olivia Egleston Phelps Stokes, *Letters and Memories of Susan and Anna Bartlett Warner* (New York: G. P. Putman's Sons, 1925), pp. 106–107.

22 Quoted in *At Home with Susan and Anna Warner: Receipts and Remembrances from 1836 to 1915*, compiled and illustrated by the Constitution Island Association, West Point, NY, 1977, p. 3.

23 Quoted in *At Home with Susan and Anna Warner: Receipts and Remembrances from 1836 to 1915*, compiled and illustrated by the Constitution Island Association, West Point, NY, 1977, p. 6.

24 Olivia Egleston Phelps Stokes, *Letters and Memories of Susan and Anna Bartlett Warner* (New York: G. P. Putman's Sons, 1925), p. 95.

25 Quoted in *A Warner Compendium*, prepared by the Constitution Island Association, 1975.

26 Olivia Egleston Phelps Stokes, *Letters and Memories of Susan and Anna Bartlett Warner* (New York: G. P. Putman's Sons, 1925), pp. 43–44.

27 Anna Walker, *The Life and Letters of Susan Warner* (New York: G. P. Putman's Sons, 1909), p. 449.

28 Olivia Egleston Phelps Stokes, *Letters and Memories of Susan and Anna Bartlett Warner* (New York: G. P. Putman's Sons, 1925), p. 43. Also Anna Walker, *The Life and Letters of Susan Warner* (New York: G. P. Putman's Sons, 1909), p. 492.

29 From a document entitled "Jesus Loves Me: Incidents from the Life of Anna Bartlett Warner," written by Charlotte Snyder and copyrighted 2004 by the Constitution Island Association, Inc.

30 Olivia Egleston Phelps Stokes, *Letters and Memories of Susan and Anna Bartlett Warner* (New York: G. P. Putman's Sons, 1925), p. 12.

31 Olivia Egleston Phelps Stokes, *Letters and Memories of Susan and Anna Bartlett Warner* (New York: G. P. Putman's Sons, 1925), p. 71.

32 Olivia Egleston Phelps Stokes, *Letters and Memories of Susan and Anna Bartlett Warner* (New York: G. P. Putman's Sons, 1925), p. 74.

33 Olivia Egleston Phelps Stokes, *Letters and Memories of Susan and Anna Bartlett Warner* (New York: G. P. Putman's Sons, 1925), p. 81.

34 Quoted in *A Warner Compendium*, prepared by the Constitution Island Association, 1975.

35 Quoted in *A Warner Compendium*, prepared by the Constitution Island Association, 1975.

36 Olivia Egleston Phelps Stokes, *Letters and Memories of Susan and Anna Bartlett Warner* (New York: G. P. Putman's Sons, 1925), p. 121.

37 Olivia Egleston Phelps Stokes, *Letters and Memories of Susan and Anna Bartlett Warner* (New York: G. P. Putman's Sons, 1925), p. 57.

38 Olivia Egleston Phelps Stokes, *Letters and Memories of Susan and Anna Bartlett Warner* (New York: G. P. Putman's Sons, 1925), p. 57.

Acknowledgements

$\mathscr{I}$ am deeply grateful for the cooperation and assistance of the United States Military Academy at West Point and by the Constitution Island Association. This book would have been impossible without their openness, hospitality, eagerness to help, and willingness to serve.

Special thanks to:

- Faith S. Herbert, archivist for the Warner files for the Constitution Island Association.
- Richard de Koster, Executive Director of the Constitution Island Association whose personal assistance was invaluable.
- Colonel and Mrs. Rick McPeak, who opened their home to us during our visit to West Point.

Anyone wanting to study this story further or visit the Warner Home is encouraged to contact the Constitution Island Association, Box 41, West Point, New York 10996, (845)446-8676, or at www.constitutionisland.org / info@constitutionisland.org.

For More Information

To learn more about other Christian songs, try these other books from pastor and author Rob Morgan:

Come Let Us Adore Him: Stories Behind the Most Cherished Christmas Hymns
Then Sings My Soul, Book 1: 150 of the World's Greatest Hymn Stories
Then Sings My Soul, Book 2: 150 of the World's Greatest Hymn Stories

www.robertjmorgan.com | www.thomasnelson.com